The Charles A. Lindbergh Coloring Book

On May 21, 1927, a 25-year-old pilot from Little Falls, Minnesota, became the first person ever to fly the Atlantic Ocean alone and non-stop from New York to Paris. He flew for 33½ hours in a single-engine airplane named "The Spirit of St. Louis."

Charles A. Lindbergh became a world hero. His flight helped make people think that airplanes might soon become a safe, fast way for ordinary people to travel.

As you color these pages, read about the life of Charles Lindbergh, one of the twentieth century's best-known flyers.

Illustrated by Mary Ellen Schutz

Copyright 1987 by The Minnesota Historical Society, St. Paul, MN 55101

ISBN   0-87351-224-3

1

Events in the life of Charles Augustus Lindbergh, Jr.

1902   Charles A. Lindbergh born in Detroit, Michigan, Feb. 4.

1906   The Lindbergh house in Little Falls is rebuilt after a fire.
          C.A. Lindbergh (Charles' father) is elected to U.S. Congress.

1918   Charles takes over running the farm.

1920   Leaves farm to attend the University of Wisconsin.

1922   Enrolls in flying classes, leaves college.

1923   Buys first airplane, a "Jenny."

1924-25 Joins Army Air Corps as a flying student.

1926   Out of the army, flies air mail between St. Louis and Chicago

1927   First solo and non-stop flight from New York to Paris.

1929   Marries Anne Morrow.

1931-33 Anne and Charles make survey flights to the Orient
          and to Europe. Anne writes books about the flights. Charles
          begins his lifelong work as an airlines advisor.

1932   The Lindberghs' baby son is kidnaped and killed.

1935-39 The Lindbergh family lives in Europe.

1941-45 Charles works as a test pilot and advisor during
          World War II.

1954   Autobiography, The Spirit of St. Louis, wins Pulitzer Prize.

1960-74 Works for the conservation of wildlife and natural
          resources.

1974   Charles A. Lindbergh dies August 26. Buried on the
          island of Maui in Hawaii.

What do you think of when someone says SUMMERTIME?!

To young Charles Lindbergh, summertime meant living along the Mississippi River in Little Falls, Minnesota.

3

Charles and his mother traveled there by train from Washington, D.C.

His father, C.A. Lindbergh, was a member of Congress in Washington, D.C. He visited the farm often.

Charles' father taught him to swim in the river.

When Charles was seven years old, he hunted with his father.

Charles liked to play with his toy soldiers in the farmhouse attic.

8

The first airplane that he ever saw in Little Falls was flying above the river behind his house.

He climbed out of the attic window for a better view.

10 Charles liked to lie in the deep grass and dream about flying.

He learned to drive at the age of 11 and often drove his father to political meetings.

He liked to drive his mother to nearby lakes for picnics.

The Lindbergh farmhouse had no electricity and no tele-
phone. Food was cooked on a wood stove, and kerosene
lamps were used at night.

Ice was cut from the Mississippi River during the winter months and stored in the icehouse.

Charles liked to figure out easier ways to haul large blocks of ice into the kitchen.

When summer was over, Charles and his mother left the farm to spend winters in Washington, D.C.

Charles made a hiding place in the kitchen wall to keep
his special things safe while they were gone.

C.A. Lindbergh liked having Charles attend meetings of Congress with him.

Charles and his mother began to spend winters at the farm in Little Falls when Charles was 16. He took charge of farming.

Charles often slept on the screened-in porch, even when the temperature was 30° below zero!

Wahgoosh, his dog, helped keep him warm!

Charles loved farming. He had lots of ideas, tried new things, and made many changes.

The "Moo Pond" that Charles built for his ducks in 1919 is still there today!

JULY - 6
1919

C.A. LINDBERGH JR.
WAHGOOSH

"Moo" is an Ojibway Indian word for dirty!

When he was 18, in 1920, Charles went to college and never spent another summer at the farm.

He didn't like college much, and after a year and a half he quit and went to flying school.

People watching were thrilled when he walked on the wings or jumped with a parachute.

He bought his first airplane in Georgia in the spring of 1923.

He flew to Minnesota and his farm in Little Falls.

In the 1920's planes were for adventure and for war.

Only a few people thought they would ever be a part of everyday life.

But when Charles Lindbergh flew to Paris non-stop in 1927, that idea changed. Many more people began to think airplanes could be useful for world travel.

Charles and his wife Anne Morrow Lindbergh made many important flights. Anne acted as co-pilot and radio operator, sending and receiving messages in Morse code.

During World War II, Charles tested fighter planes in the Pacific.

Charles loved the outdoors and worked to save endangered animals, clean up air pollution, and set aside wilderness areas.

Some of the animals he helped save are pictured here.

Monkey Eating Eagle

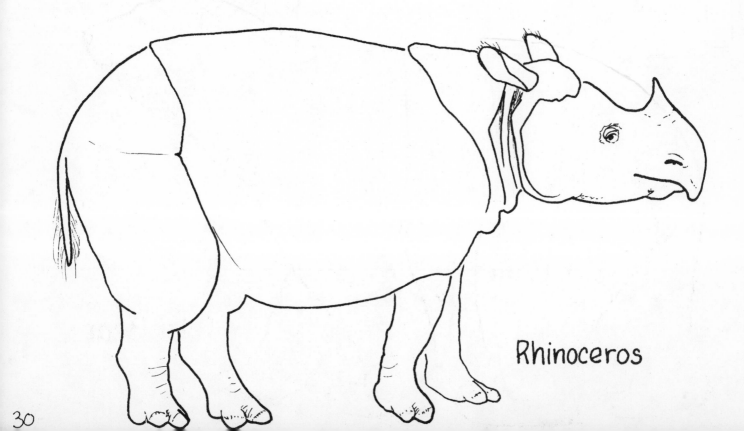

Rhinoceros

Red Wolf

Polar Bear

".....where civilization is most advanced,
few birds exist. I realize if I had to choose,
I would rather have birds than airplanes."

Charles A. Lindbergh